Introduction

It is three years since the appearance of *More Instant Art for the Church Magazine*, but — as we hope this new book will show — we have not been wholly idle in the intervening time! 'Book Three' has been compiled with the needs of our users very much in mind, since thanks to those who have taken the trouble to write to us with constructive criticism and suggestions, we have a good idea of what people want. So we are now able to offer a fresh collection of 46 pages of high quality photocopiable artwork for use in church publications of various kinds.

Flexibility/versatility

From the examples which have been received at Palm Tree, we know that people have found many different ways of using 'instant art' material. By enlarging and reducing items, deleting unwanted portions, or otherwise adapting what is printed, editors and others have found ingenious ways adding to the list of 'known uses of instant art material'!

Hints on layout

More Instant Art for the Church Magazine contains some helpful hints on the general principles of design and layout, and John Cole's book *How to Produce a Church Magazine* is an invaluable source of more detailed guidance on all practical matters concerned with church publishing.

Copyright

The material in this book is copyright-free, *provided that* it is used for the purpose for which the book is intended. The usual copyright restrictions apply to any use for *commercial* purposes.

Readers' Responses

The 'instant art' series has been developing in response to ideas and suggestions from people who have used earlier titles. We would welcome any comments you might wish to make on existing books, and ideas for new additions to the list are always carefully considered.

Contributors

Bridget Andrews
Arthur Baker
Juliette Clarke
John Cole
Harriet Dell
Karen Holford
Jill Kelbrick
Mary McCullough
Roy Mitchell
Lily Rainbird
Susan Sayers

instant
art for the CHURCH MAGAZINE

Book Three

First published in Great Britain
© 1990 Palm Tree Press
(see note about copyright in introduction).

ISBN 0 86208 143 2
Palm Tree Press
Rattlesden
Bury St. Edmunds
Suffolk
IP30 0SZ

Cover by Roy Mitchell
Typesetting by Typestylers, Ipswich, Suffolk
Printed in Great Britain by The Five Castles Press Limited

Mission is . . . organising the cubs to clear snow for the old folk.

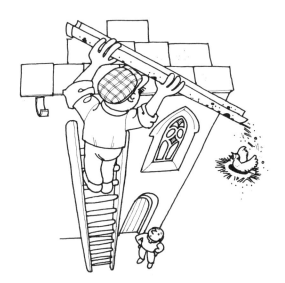

Mission is . . . spending £1,000 repairing the church gutters, thus saving £10,000 eradicating dry rot.

Mission is . . . making friends with vandals.

Mission is . . . battling with bureaucrats.

Mission is . . . cleaning up after the youth club disco.

Mission is . . . letting the local rock group rehearse in the church hall.

He will reign for ever.

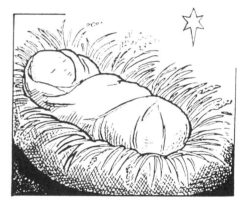

God sent his own Son.

Joy to the world.

Christ has come to earth.

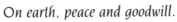

On earth, peace and goodwill.

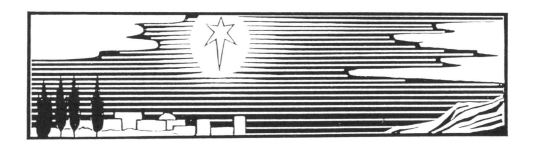

Candelight service.

RESURRECTION

Celebrate
The Victory
he lives!
let us rejoice

Good Friday

He is not here –
He has risen !

He Suffered

REJOICE IN THE RISEN LORD

He Lives!

Darkness has not over come us

The Lord has risen indeed

Holy Week

EASTER
IS A PROMISE

In God I trust

COME HOLY SPIRIT

ALLELUIA
CHRIST IS RISEN

AMEN

EASTER

Come and Praise Him

hosanna!

Christ died that we may Live

Jesus is Lord

Hallelujah! what a Saviour

it is finished

LENT

The Lord is good

Ascension Day

Truly this was the son of God

ASH WEDNESDAY

Palm Sunday

IMMANUEL

MAUNDY THURSDAY

Do not be anxious.

With God all things
are possible.

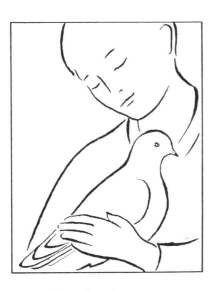

Peace is not a season,
it is a way of life.

Love God,
love neighbour.

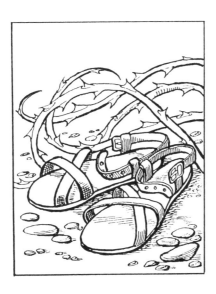

Go out
into all the world.

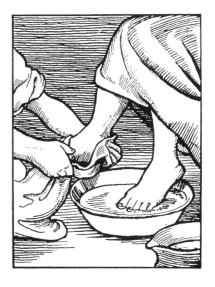

We also will serve
the Lord.

Come into his house
with praise.

Love your enemies.

I am the Way, the Truth,
and the Life.

Hosanna!

Do you love me?
Feed my sheep.

Every good and perfect gift
is from above.

CROSSWORD

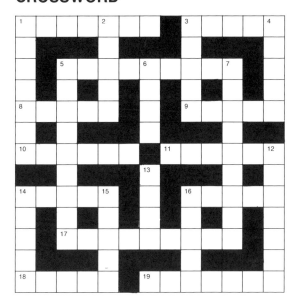

Clues Across

1. Paul's fellow worker. Acts 16 (7)
3. A weapon of warfare (5)
5. At the wedding at Cana these were filled with water. John 2 (9)
8. These are numbered. Matthew 10:30 (5)
9. Church council (5)
10. These hold no terror for those who do right. Romans 13:3 (6)
11. We put bits into the . . . . . . of horses to make them obey. James 3:3 (6)
14. Chief of religious order (5)
16. Slow moving mollusc (5)
17. One humped camel (9)
18. A dealer in purple cloth. Acts 16:14 (5)
19. A city of the Amorites. Numbers 21:26 (7)

Clues Down

1. Nicodemus called Jesus one. John 3:2 (7)
2. Paul wrote a letter to this Gentile (5)
3. ''Who is worthy to break the . . . . . and open the scroll?'' Revelations 5:2 (5)
4. Shepherd boy who became king of Israel. 2 Samuel 5:3 (5)
5. Elijah was taken to heaven in this. 2 Kings 2:11 (9)
6. City founded on the Tiber river (4)
7. Praise God here. Psalm 150:1 (9)
12. King of Israel who asked for wisdom. 2 Chronicles 1:10 (7)
13. Book in the New Testament and brother of James (4)
14. Jewel of great value. Matthew 13:45 (5)
15. Servant girl who answered the door to Peter. Acts 12:13 (5)
16. God made these on the fourth day. Genesis 1 (5)

Suggestion
Print the solution upside down or on another page.

SOLUTION

Across 1. Timothy 3. Sword 5. Waterjars 8. Hairs 9. Synod 10. Rulers 11. Mouths 14. Prior 16. Snail 17. Dromedary 18. Lydia 19. Heshbon

Down 1. Teacher 2. Titus 3. Seals 4. David 5. Whirlwind 6. Rome 7. Sanctuary 12. Solomon 13. Jude 14. Pearl 15. Rhoda 16. Stars

---

FITWORD   ''WOMEN OF THE BIBLE''

3 LETTERS
EVE

4 LETTERS
ANNA
LEAH
MARY
RUTH

5 LETTERS
NAOMI
RHODA
SARAH

6 LETTERS
DORCAS
ESTHER
EUNICE
HANNAH
JOANNA
MARTHA
PHOEBE
SALOME

7 LETTERS
BERNICE
DELILAH
REBEKAH

8 LETTERS
SAPPHIRA

9 LETTERS
BATHSHEBA
PRISCILLA

See if you can fit these words into their correct positions in the diagram. Find your own starter for this puzzle.

CROSSWORD

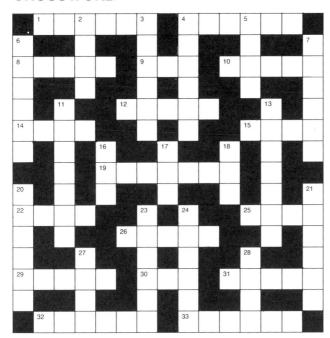

Clues Across

1. A piece of armour in Ephesians 6. (6)
4. King when Daniel was put into the lions den. Daniel 6 (6)
8. His sin at Jericho caused defeat at Ai. Joshua 7 (5)
9. Grandfather of King Saul. 1 Chronicles 8:33 (3)
10. Peter stayed here with Simon. Acts 9:43 (5)
12. Tree for which 11 down was famous. Psalm 92:12 (5)
14. God put man into this garden. Genesis 2 (4)
15. Guided the Magi to the child Jesus. (4)
19. This king gave Joseph his signet ring. Genesis 41:42 (7)
22. A minor prophet. (4)
25. Most southerly of the Philistine cities. (4)
26. In the temple Jesus found men selling these. John 2. (5)
29. ''I am the . . . . . and the Omega'' says the Lord God. Revelations 1:8 (5)
30. Jesus told a paralytic man ''Get up, take your . . . and go home.'' Mark 2:11 (3)
31. Son of Cain. Genesis 4 (5)
32. A village 7 miles from Jerusalem. Luke 24:13 (6)
33. He set a riddle for his enemies. Judges 14 (6)

Clues Down

2. Wife of Jacob. Genesis 29 (4)
3. Peter stayed in Joppa with Simon a . . . . . . Acts 9:43 (6)
4. She was always doing good. Acts 9:36 (6)
5. Elisha made this float. 2 Kings 6:6 (4)
6. One of the gates of the city of Jerusalem. Nehemiah 3 (6)
7. Town south east of the Sea of Galilee. (6)
11. See 12 across. (7)
13. This glory will far outweigh all. 2 Corinthians 4:17 (7)
16. Joshua sent men to Ai to do this. Joshua 7:2 (3)
17. Noah built one. Genesis 6 (3)
18. The feminine pronoun of the third person. (3)
20. Mother of Samuel. 1 Samuel 1:20 (6)
21. King of Israel. 1 Kings 15:16 (6)
23. Apostle who doubted the resurrection. John 20 (6)
24. Successor of Felix. Acts 24:27 (6)
27. Son of Noah. Genesis 5:32 (4)
28. Creatures of little strength. Proverbs 30:25 (4)

SOLUTION

Across 1. Helmet 4. Darius 8. Achan 9. Ner 10. Joppa 12. Cedar 14. Eden 15. Star 19. Pharaoh 22. Amos 25. Gaza 26. Sheep 29. Alpha 30. Mat 31. Enoch 32. Emmaus 33. Samson

Down 2. Leah 3. Tanner 4. Dorcas 5. Iron 6. Valley 7. Gadara 11. Lebanon 13. Eternal 16. Spy 17. Ark 18. She 20. Hannah 21. Baasha 23. Thomas 24. Festus 27. Shem 28. Ants

> Suggestion
> Print the solution upside down or on another page.

FITWORD   ''BIBLICAL CITIES''

4 LETTERS
ARAD
ROME
TYRE

5 LETTERS
ERECH
SODOM

6 LETTERS
BOZRAH
CYRENE
RABBAH
THEBES

7 LETTERS
BABYLON
MEGIDDO
MEMPHIS

8 LETTERS
ASHKELON
DAMASCUS
MITYLENE
GOMORRAH

9 LETTERS
ASHTAROTH
JERUSALEM

10 LETTERS
HIERAPOLIS

See if you can fit these words into their correct positions in the diagram. Find your own starter for this puzzle.

CROSSWORD

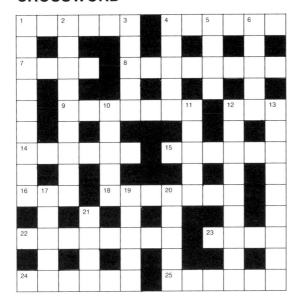

Clues Across

1. The plant family to which onions, garlic and leeks belong (6)
4. Tomb or place of special holy memory (6)
7. ''Just as man is destined to die . . . .'' Hebrews 9:27 (4)
8. ''At the resurrection people will neither marry or be given in . . . . .'' Matthew 22:30 (8)
9. First book of the Old Testament (7)
12. Wife to Adam (3)
14. Mediterranean island where John had the vision of Revelations (6)
15. Beautiful daughter of Laban, and mother of Joseph (6)
16. Beast of burden (3)
18. Part 1 of the ''Divine Comedy'' by Dante (7)
22. French Protestant of the 17th and 18th century (8)
23. ''So if God gave them the same . . . as he gave us . . .'' Acts 11:17 (4)
24. Birthplace of Paul (6)
25. Singer and poet, famous for the song ''Imagine'' (6)

Clues Down

1. Sacred writings not included in the Old Testament (9)
2. Roofed church-yard gates (4-5)
3. Abraham camped under the oak trees of this place. Genesis 13:18 (5)
4. Turkish caravanserai (5)
5. ''I will . . . . down bread from Heaven'' Exodus 16:4 (4)
6. Desert of southern Israel (5)
10. Mother-in-law of Ruth (5)
11. ''A . . . . . way led up to the middle level'' 1 Kings 6:8 (5)
12. Native of Addis Ababa, the Cush of the Old Testament (9)
13. ''The eyes of your heart may be . . . . ed'' Ephesians 1:18 (9)
17. Buddhist dome-shaped memorial shrine (5)
19. A church office, originally for the ninth hour (5)
20. Laud and praise (5)
21. Religious sisters (4)

SOLUTION

Across 1. Allium 4. Shrine 7. Once 8. Marriage 9. Genesis 12. Eve 14. Patmos 15. Rachel 16. Ass 18. Inferno 22. Huguenot 23. Gift 24. Tarsus 25. Lennon

Down 1. Apocrypha 2. Lych-gates 3. Mamre 4. Serai 5. Rain 6. Negev 10. Naomi 11. Stair 12. Ethiopian 13. Enlighten 17. Stupa 19. Nones 20. Extol 21. Nuns

Suggestion
Print the solution upside down or on another page.

SEARCHWORD
''THE PROPHETS''

Z	I	P	H	K	U	K	K	A	B	A	H	J
K	A	B	Z	I	H	A	I	D	A	B	O	O
E	G	A	M	E	C	H	D	H	A	C	I	M
Z	G	K	A	L	C	A	I	Z	J	O	N	E
E	A	U	K	A	N	H	S	H	U	O	A	L
K	H	E	L	I	S	H	A	B	K	P	E	H
I	Z	A	E	K	K	I	I	R	H	L	N	L
E	M	L	B	O	N	A	A	E	I	H	A	J
L	E	U	M	A	S	H	H	J	E	A	T	E
S	D	I	H	A	Z	O	A	Z	K	N	H	R
B	O	P	H	E	S	H	E	I	E	O	A	D
O	E	M	Z	E	M	U	H	A	N	J	N	A
Z	D	I	A	H	H	A	I	M	E	R	E	J

WORD LIST

AMOS	HABAKKUK	JOEL	NATHAN
DANIEL	HAGGAI	JONAH	OBADIAH
ELIJAH	HOSEA	MALACHI	SAMUEL
ELISHA	ISAIAH	MICAH	ZECHARIAH
EZEKIEL	JEREMIAH	NAHUM	ZEPHANIAH

CROSSWORD

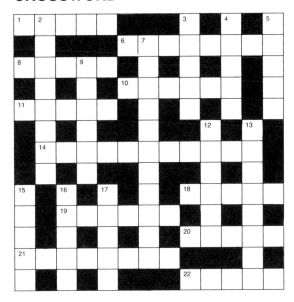

Clues Across

1. Country famed for its gold. 1 Kings 9:28 (5)
6. Church festival celebrated on 6th January (8)
8. Mother-in-law of Ruth (5)
10. Great warrior and nephew of David. 1 Chronicles 2:16 (6)
11. Employing (5)
14. One of the twelve apostles (11)
18. "Oh Lord, ... I am your servant" Psalm 116:16 (5)
19. A clergyman (6)
20. A Caananite city in the north of Israel. Joshua 11 (5)
21. Covered arcade forming part of a monastery (8)
22. Symbol of the Christian faith (5)

Clues Down

2. Words of thanksgiving to the Lord (6,2)
3. Algerian cavalryman (5)
4. Underground chamber with arched roof (5)
5. Woman described as a "dealer in purple cloth" in Acts 16:14-15 (5)
7. The two weeks preceding Easter (11)
9. Word or phrase repeated inwardly in meditation (6)
12. City and port mentioned in Revelation 1:11 (6)
13. Birds mentioned in Psalm 84:3 (7)
15. A descendant of Adam's son, Seth. Genesis 5:22 (5)
16. "Trouble Valley" near Jericho. Joshua 7:24 (5)
17. Father of King David (5)

SOLUTION

Across 1. Ophir 6. Epiphany 8. Naomi
10. Asahel 11. Using 14. Bartholomew
18. Truly 19. Cleric 20. Hazor 21. Cloister
22. Cross

Down 2. Praise Be 3. Spahi 4. Vault
5. Lydia 7. Passiontide 9. Mantra
12. Smyrna 13. Swallows 15. Enoch
16. Achor 17. Jesse

> Suggestion
> Print the solution upside down
> or on another page.

SEARCHWORD
"ANIMAL, VEGETABLE AND
MINERAL OF THE BIBLE"

S	E	A	I	C	A	C	A	M	N	O	E	G	I	P
I	R	P	R	E	P	P	O	C	G	E	P	R	I	A
L	W	O	R	R	A	P	S	P	A	O	N	A	N	F
V	P	E	V	I	L	O	A	S	Z	M	E	I	E	W
L	A	R	C	Z	M	Y	R	R	E	E	V	L	V	I
A	E	A	D	L	O	G	Y	M	T	E	T	A	C	L
K	N	O	I	L	N	L	T	A	A	R	F	L	O	L
C	A	M	P	O	D	E	N	G	Y	Y	I	M	P	O
A	L	E	M	A	C	A	L	M	Y	R	T	D	P	W
J	C	L	E	O	R	E	E	D	L	T	A	O	G	N
S	P	A	R	G	T	D	Y	P	M	Q	E	O	L	E
H	F	O	E	W	N	E	A	Z	Y	U	F	E	I	V
E	L	M	P	O	P	L	A	R	R	A	D	E	C	A
E	O	A	R	V	M	R	E	V	L	I	S	I	G	R
P	W	I	N	E	P	I	G	E	L	L	E	Z	A	G

WORD LIST

ACACIA	FIG	MYRTLE	QUAIL
ALMOND	GAZELLE	OLIVE	RAVEN
CAMEL	GOAT	PALM	SHEEP
CEDAR	GOLD	PARTRIDGE	SILVER
COPPER	IRON	PIGEON	SPARROW
DEER	JACKAL	POMEGRANATE	VINE
EAGLE	LEOPARD	POPLAR	WILLOW
	LION		WOLF

CROSSWORD

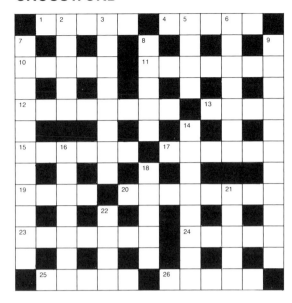

Clues Across

1. Leonardo da . . . . . painter of the "Last Supper" (5)
4. This diseased man was healed in Luke 17:11-19 (5)
10. King of Moab in the time of the Judges. Judges 3:12-26 (5)
11. Mediterranean island (7)
12. Members or knights of a religious and military order (8)
13. Hindu women's garment (4)
15. "Will you not . . . . . . us again" Psalm 85:6 (6)
17. Place 12 miles from Jerusalem where Jacob dreamed of a staircase to Heaven (6)
19. Shelled fruit of Genesis 43:11 (4)
20. An older name for a hired hand. John 10:12 (8)
23. Archangel described in Daniel as the guardian of the Jewish people (7)
24. Images of gods which are objects of worship (5)
25. Heavenly being (5)
26. "But Paul . . . . Silas and left" Acts 15:40 (5)

Down

2. The Muslim religion (5)
3. The meeting of cardinals to elect a pope (8)
5. Teacher and preacher of the law in the Old Testament (4)
6. Tombstone inscription (7)
7. Book of the Old Testament (11)
8. "It will bring . . . . and derision" Ezekiel 23:32 (5)
9. One who studies the saints (11)
14. King of Judah 716-687 BC (8)
16. The papal authority (7)
18. Holy book of Christianity (5)
21. Sacred paintings and mosaics in Eastern churches (5)
22. Main body of a church (4)

SOLUTION

Across 1. Vinci 4. Leper 10. Eglon
11. Corsica 12. Templars 13. Sari 15. Revive
17. Bethel 19. Nuts 20. Hireling 23. Michael
24. Idols 25. Angel 26. Chose

Down 2. Islam 3. Conclave 5. Ezra
6. Epitaph 7. Deuteronomy 8. Scorn
9. Hagiologist 14. Hezekiah 16. Vatican
18. Bible 21. Icons 22. Nave

Suggestion
Print the solution upside down
or on another page.

BIBLE QUIZ SEARCHWORD

T	I	M	R	E	V	O	S	S	A	P	A
C	N	E	V	A	H	R	I	A	F	C	M
I	B	Y	A	W	A	R	A	C	I	R	A
T	A	S	U	S	R	A	T	N	A	V	L
P	B	D	B	N	A	M	O	H	T	S	E
O	Y	R	A	O	R	L	P	I	S	H	K
N	L	A	B	L	A	I	M	A	T	D	I
Y	O	P	Y	S	T	O	M	O	O	O	T
S	N	O	S	O	T	A	B	V	N	R	E
R	B	E	P	H	R	A	E	A	C	D	S
A	H	L	Y	I	N	S	A	C	R	O	D
T	M	H	A	L	E	S	U	H	T	E	M

1. City on the Euphrates. 2 Kings 24:1
2. Flowering tree of Numbers 17:8
3. Mountain on which Noah's ark came to rest — Genesis 8:4
4. Remembered as the oldest man who ever lived
5. Paul's birthplace
6. Egyptian official who bought Joseph as a slave
7. Small port in Crete at which Paul called on the way to Rome Acts 27:7-8
8. Capital of the northern kingdom of Israel
9. Nomadic tribe at the time of the exodus. Exodus 17:8-13
10. Spice from Isaiah 28:25
11. Name given to the first three gospels
12. Animal of the cat family mentioned in Isaiah 11:6
13. City which was the capital of the Roman province of Macedonia. Acts 17:1
14. Owner of a vineyard next to King Ahab's palace. 1 Kings 21
15. A Christian from Lystra who was a friend and helper of Paul. Acts 16:1
16. Great Jewish feast
17. Birds that were sold in the temple courts for sacrifice
18. A Christian woman who helped the poor by making clothes from them. Acts 9:36-41

SOLUTION

1. Babylon 2. Almond 3. Ararat 4. Methuselah
5. Tarsus 6. Potiphar 7. Fair Haven 8. Samaria
9. Amalekites 10. Caraway 11. Synoptic
12. Leopard 13. Thessalonica 14. Naboth
15. Timothy 16. Passover 17. Doves 18. Dorcas

SEARCHWORD
"THE JOURNEYS OF PAUL"

S	P	A	T	L	A	M	A	I	L	A	T	T	A	S
A	R	T	S	Y	L	P	E	E	S	O	S	S	A	Y
O	A	I	C	U	E	L	E	S	E	S	U	C	M	R
R	T	S	M	O	P	A	P	H	U	B	A	U	A	A
T	H	Y	C	H	T	N	I	R	O	C	I	S	L	E
E	R	I	P	H	R	P	Y	C	I	N	A	D	T	P
A	L	N	E	H	O	S	S	N	O	M	N	R	H	H
E	O	N	R	B	I	H	O	C	A	Y	T	C	Y	E
S	S	R	G	O	T	L	I	R	S	R	I	O	E	S
S	I	M	A	L	A	S	I	H	O	H	O	R	B	U
N	O	D	I	S	R	A	O	P	H	T	C	M	R	S
H	P	U	S	T	S	D	E	S	P	N	H	R	E	A
P	A	E	R	A	U	T	T	A	A	I	M	Y	D	H
R	H	O	D	E	S	S	U	R	P	Y	C	A	E	T
T	A	E	O	R	E	B	A	E	R	A	S	E	A	C

WORD LIST

ANTIOCH	CYPRUS	PAPHOS	SELEUCIA
ASSOS	DERBE	PERGA	SIDON
ATHENS	EPHESUS	PHILIPPI	SYRACUSE
ATTALIA	ICONIUM	RHODES	TARSUS
BEROEA	LYSTRA	ROME	THESSALONICA
CAESAREA	MALTA	SALAMIS	TROAS
CORINTH	MYRA	SAMARIA	

Suggestion
Print the solution upside down
or on another page.

BIBLE QUIZ SEARCHWORD

N	E	G	S	A	H	P	A	I	A	C	P
V	E	N	I	R	U	O	B	M	A	T	O
S	M	N	G	P	O	M	E	G	H	L	M
A	L	E	E	O	D	C	L	C	R	A	E
L	A	P	L	S	M	I	U	D	N	Z	G
L	Z	V	G	I	Z	E	R	B	A	B	R
I	A	E	A	N	T	A	R	Y	I	A	A
C	R	G	E	A	Z	A	B	L	N	T	N
S	U	E	T	I	Y	E	L	R	A	B	A
I	S	N	L	V	N	A	D	R	O	J	T
R	E	Y	A	I	C	U	E	L	E	S	E
P	T	A	H	P	A	H	S	O	H	E	J

1. Old name for the Mediterranean island where Paul was shipwrecked.
2. High-Priest of Jerusalem AD 18-36, son-in-law of Annas.
3. Unfaithful wife of the prophet Hosea.
4. Brother of Martha and Mary who lived in Bethany.
5. Cereal crop from 2 Samuel 17:28.
6. Port of Antioch in Syria from which Paul and Barnabas set sail.
7. Biblical measurement of length from elbow to finger-tip.
8. The commandments were given to Moses at the foot of this mountain.
9. Bird mentioned in Psalm 103:5.
10. Fruit carved into the pillars of Solomon's temple. 1 Kings 7:20.
11. Tentmaker from Acts 18:1-3.
12. Desert of southern Israel.
13. Musical instrument of Exodus 15:20.
14. Reptile of Proverbs 30:28.
15. King of Judah, 870-848 BC.
16. River in which John the Baptist baptised Jesus.
17. First five books of the Old Testament.
18. Town where Jesus restored the widow's son to life. Luke 7:11-15.

SOLUTION

1. Melita 2. Caiaphas 3. Gomer 4. Lazarus
5. Barley 6. Seleucia 7. Cubit 8. Sinai 9. Eagle
10. Pomegranate 11. Priscilla 12. Negev
13. Tambourine 14. Lizard 15. Jehoshaphat
16. Jordan 17. Pentateuch 18. Nain

SEARCHWORD/BIBLE QUIZ SEARCHWORD

"I HEAR HE USED TO BE AN OLYMPIC ATHLETE..."

"WHAT DO YOU MEAN, YOU'RE BORED?"

"WELL, I SUPPOSE THIS RULES OUT THE 'HALLELUIAH CHORUS'..."

"I DON'T CARE IF HEMLINES ARE UP THIS SEASON, BROTHER RANDOLPH— GET RID OF IT!"

"ACTUALLY, I DON'T THINK I'M GOING TO LIKE IT HERE— I'M TERRIFIED OF HEIGHTS..."

"THE HOURS ARE LONG, THE PAY'S LOUSY, BUT THE LONG-TERM PROSPECTS ARE OUT OF THIS WORLD..."

"PERHAPS I COULD EXPLAIN AGAIN WHAT I MEANT BY 'SHARED LEADERSHIP'..."

"I TOLD YOU THE CHURCH COUNCIL MEETINGS WERE LIVELY, DIDN'T I?"

"DO WE WANT ANY DOUBLE-GLAZING?"

"I'M 'KNUCKLES', AND I'M IN CHARGE OF THE OFFERTORY PLATE..."

PARISH MAGAZINE

CHURCH NEWSLETTER

EASTER

SPRING

EASTER

SPRING

EASTER

SPRING

SUMMER

SUMMER

SUMMER

PARISH MAGAZINE

CHURCH MAGAZINE

NEWS LETTER

PARISH MAGAZINE

CHURCH MAGAZINE

NEWSLETTER

AUTUMN

AUTUMN

AUTUMN

WINTER

CHRISTMAS

CHRISTMAS

WINTER

WINTER

CHRISTMAS

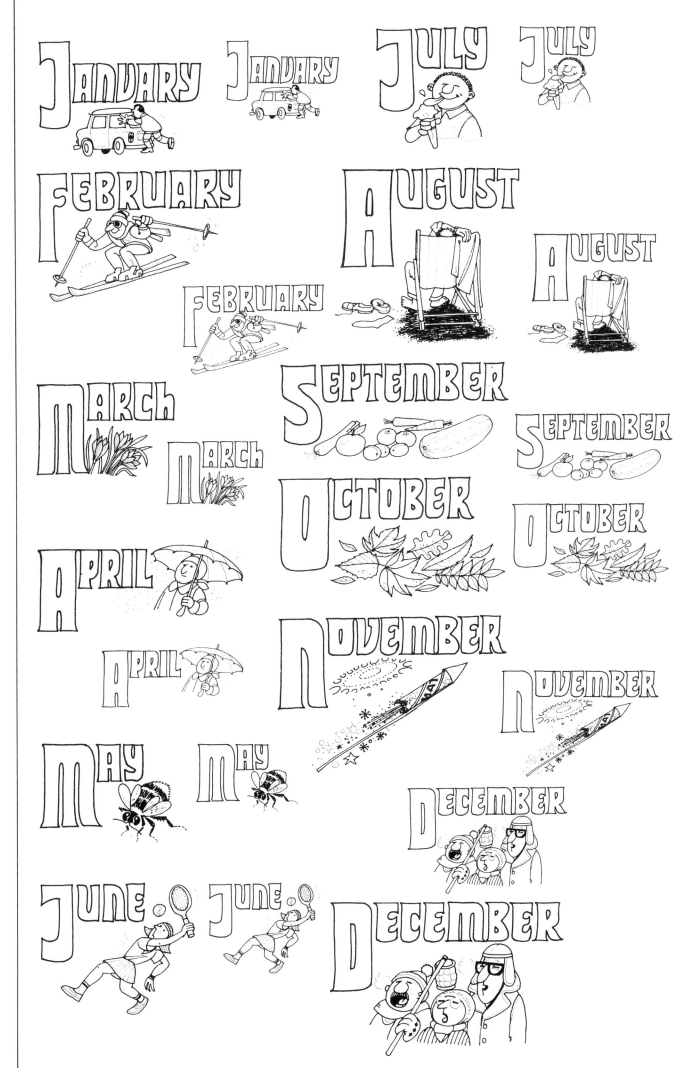

TREES, PLANTS and FLOWERS OF THE BIBLE

Key to the drawings on the opposite page, with Bible references:

1. Myrtle
   One of the leafy plants used by the Jews for making booths (or tabernacles) at the Feast of the Tabernacles, as a reminder of their exodus from Egypt (Leviticus 23:40-43; Nehemiah 8:15). The prophet Isaiah envisaged myrtle as one day replacing the prickly brier of the desert (Isaiah 41:19; 55:13). Esther's name, Hadassah, was derived from the Hebrew word for myrtle (Esther 2:7).

2. Pomegranate
   Exodus 28:33-34; Deuteronomy 8:8.
   Its Hebrew name, 'rimmon' was applied to locations (Numbers 33:19-20) and people (2 Samuel 4:2).

3. Vine
   e.g. Genesis 9:20; Psalm 104:15; Proverbs 20:1; Matthew 26:27-29; 1 Corinthians 11:25; Isaiah 5:1-10; John 15:1.

4. Mustard seed and plant
   Mark 4:30-32; Luke 17:6.

5. Olive
   Matthew 26:36; 1 Samuel 10:1.

6. Flax
   2 Chronicles 1:16; Isaiah 19:9; Ezekiel 27:7, 16; Joshua 2:1-6.

7. Fig
   1 Samuel 25:18; 1 Chronicles 12:40; Hosea 9:10; Amos 8:1-2; Zechariah 3:10; John 1:48; Matthew 7:16; 21:13; Luke 13:6ff; Luke 21:29-30; Mark 11:13, 20.

8. Cumin
   Matthew 23:23

9. Dill
   Matthew 23:23

10. Hyssop
    A bunch of 'hyssop' was used for sprinkling blood on the door lintels and posts at the time of Passover (Exodus 12:22); and during the sacrifices in the Tabernacle (Leviticus 14:4, 6, 22; Numbers 19:6, 18). Psalm 51:7.

11. Barley
    The scriptures often refer to barley as a crop (Exodus 9:31), as grain (Ezekiel 4:9) and as loaves (John 6:9). Ruth 1:22.

12. Palm leaf
    Deuteronomy 34:3; Numbers 33:9; Judges 4:5; John 12:13; Matthew 21:8.

13. Papyrus
    Isaiah 18:2

14. Lily
    Hosea 14:5; Matthew 6:28.

15. Cedar of Lebanon
    1 Kings 5; 2 Chronicles 2; Amos 2:9; Hosea 14:5.

Happy are those who are humble; they will receive what God has promised.

Be happy and glad, for a great reward is kept for you in Heaven.

Happy are those who are merciful to others; God will be merciful to them!

Happy are those who know they are spiritually poor; the Kingdom of Heaven belongs to them!

Happy are those who mourn; God will comfort them!

Happy are those whose greatest desire is to do what God requires; God will satisfy them fully!

Happy are those who work for peace; God will call them his children!

Happy are those who are persecuted because they do what God requires; the Kingdom of Heaven belongs to them!

Happy are the pure in heart; they will see God.

Happy are you when people insult you and persecute you and tell all kinds of lies against you because you are my followers.

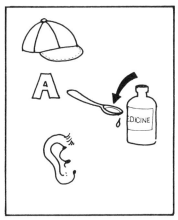

CAPPADOCIA. ACTS 2:9

PICTOGRAMS

PEOPLE AND PLACES IN THE BIBLE

THE CLUES ARE NOT INTENDED TO GIVE ACCURATE SPELLINGS, BUT TO INDICATE THE SOUNDS OF THE NAMES.

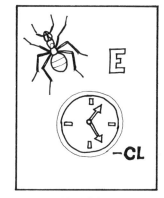

ANTIOCH.
ACTS 6:5

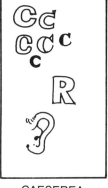

CAESEREA.
ACTS 8:40

SOLOMON'S TEMPLE.
(SEW-LEMONS) 1 KINGS 3:1

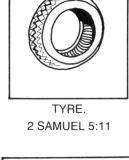

TYRE.
2 SAMUEL 5:11

ICONIUM.
ACTS 13:51

BEERSHEBA.
GENESIS 21:14

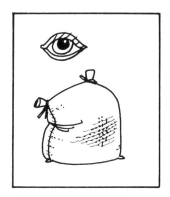

PHILIPPI.
ACTS 16:12

LYSTRA.
ACTS 14:6

TIBERIAS. JOHN 6:23

ISAAC. GENESIS 18:1-15

GALILEE. MATTHEW 4:13

ABEL. GENESIS 4:2

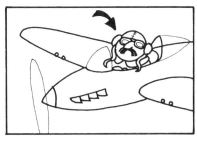

PILATE. JOHN 27:2

DEAD SEA (SALT SEA).
GENESIS 14:3

HOSEA.

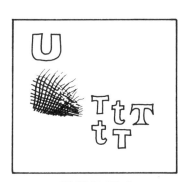

EUPHRATES.
GENESIS 2:14

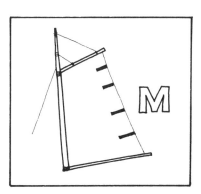

SALEM (JERUSALEM).
GENESIS 14:18

PICTOGRAMS

PEOPLE AND PLACES IN THE BIBLE

THE CLUES ARE NOT INTENDED TO
GIVE ACCURATE SPELLINGS, BUT
TO INDICATE THE SOUNDS OF THE
NAMES.

MOUNT SINAI.
EXODUS 3:1

BATHSHEBA. 2 SAMUEL 11:3

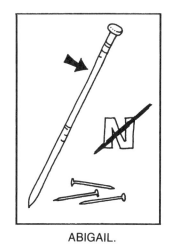

ABIGAIL.
1 SAMUEL 25:3

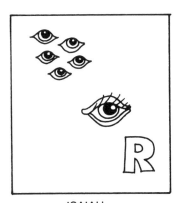

ISAIAH.
2 KINGS 19:2

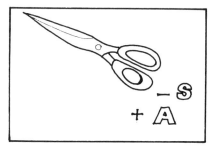

SISERA. JUDGES 4:2

OBED. RUTH 4:17

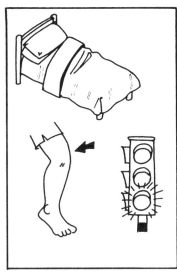

ABEDNEGO. DANIEL 1:7

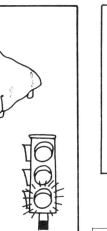

ELIJAH. 1 KINGS 17:1

JACOB. GENESIS 25:19

PICTOGRAMS

PEOPLE AND PLACES IN THE BIBLE

THE CLUES ARE NOT INTENDED TO GIVE ACCURATE SPELLINGS, BUT TO INDICATE THE SOUNDS OF THE NAMES.

MATTHEW. MARK 3:18

POTIPHAR. GENESIS 37:36

ESAU. GENESIS 25:21

SEARCHWORD

A	S	E	G	L	E	G	N	A
B	T	U	T	C	Q	K	W	Z
F	O	P	N	E	M	O	W	O
O	N	F	B	D	D	A	A	D
U	E	S	E	E	A	R	L	Y
N	U	A	L	V	W	Y	I	B
D	D	L	R	H	A	F	V	M
G	O	Y	C	M	Y	L	E	O
R	J	E	S	U	S	N	X	T

Very EARLY on SUNDAY morning the WOMEN went to the TOMB. They FOUND the huge STONE had been ROLLED AWAY. An ANGEL told them that JESUS was no longer DEAD. He was ALIVE!

JESUS is alive!

So we give each other as a sign of

HAPPY EASTER

Harvest is a good time to say a great BIG:

when you bring your gift to God . . .

and then remember you are angry with your brother . . .

leave your gift at the altar . . .

go and make it up with your brother . . .

and then come and offer your gift!

HARVEST

A good neighbour story that Jesus told. Tell it in your own words.

Which one was being a good neighbour ? Luke 10:25-34

NEIGHBOURS

Crack the code and find two rules Jesus gave us for living his way

◇	○	⬢	▽	◠	◡	8	⌢	⌇	▭	⌇	◉	⬭	⊕	◁	▷
A	B	D	E	F	G	H	I	L	N	R	O	S	U	V	Y

Rule No 1

Rule No 2

LEAD US NOT INTO TEMPTATION

Colour in the dotted spaces to see how we can resist temptation

Adam and Eve were tempted

And did they give in!

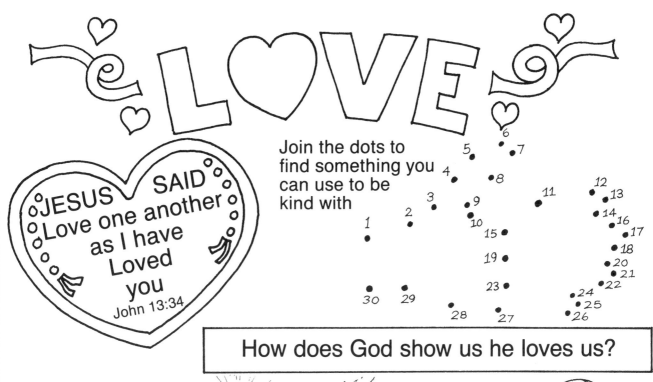

LOVE

JESUS SAID
Love one another
as I have
Loved
you
John 13:34

Join the dots to find something you can use to be kind with

How does God show us he loves us?

He gives everyone ☀ and 🌧 and a beautiful 🌍.
He comforts us when we are 😞 and is happy when we are 😊.
He makes 🌾 grow so we can make 🍞. When we are not sure which ⌐ to go, he helps us choose wisely. He loves us ALL — every person is special.

IN THE BEGINNING GOD CREATED THE

UNIVERSE!

(AND IT WAS VERY GOOD)

Draw green circles round plants, blue squares round animals, red triangles round planets.

And our job is to look after it all!

RHINOCEROS   ROSE   MARS   SQUIRREL

SATURN

RHUBARB

MERCURY   MARIGOLD

CACTUS   MONKEY

ELEPHANT

URANUS

Who lives in this hole?

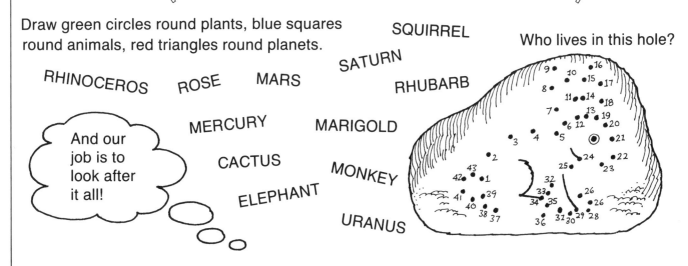

What's your name?

NAME.............................

Your name is special — it tells everyone who you are. Try matching these names with their meanings

OFFICIAL DATE STAMP

ADAM   Pleasant   judge   a rock   PETER

SARAH   DANIEL   princess   NAOMI   mankind

A PICTURE TO COLOUR

God called Moses to lead his people

HEALING

How can these men get their friend through the crowd so Jesus can heal him?
Luke 5:17-26

Colour in the dotted spaces to find out.

WHEN [   ] CAME
PEOPLE [   ] TO JESUS
MANY WHO WERE [   ] AND
JESUS [   ] THEM [   ]

Mark 1:32-34

Why did he bother?

Because he loves us

healed   ill   all   evening   brought

SIGNS AND MIRACLES

Signs of God's love

Y = Yellow
G = Green
Bl = Blue
P = Purple
O = Orange
B = Brown

One small boy offered   and

and Jesus used his gift so that 5000 people had plenty to eat!

Jesus was ready to give his life up for us. So the cross reminds us of how much he loves us.

At Cana, Jesus went to a wedding. There was not enough wine. So Jesus told the servants to fill the pots with water. What happened when he poured out the water?

Why follow Jesus?

He doesn't just KNOW the way — He IS the way!

GREED
LOVE
RICHES
POWER

Which way leads to lasting happiness?

HEAVEN
LIFETIME

Colour in the spotty fish to leave the names of two brothers who Jesus called to follow Him.

The men were ☐☐☐☐☐☐ and ☐☐☐☐☐

The good Shepherd

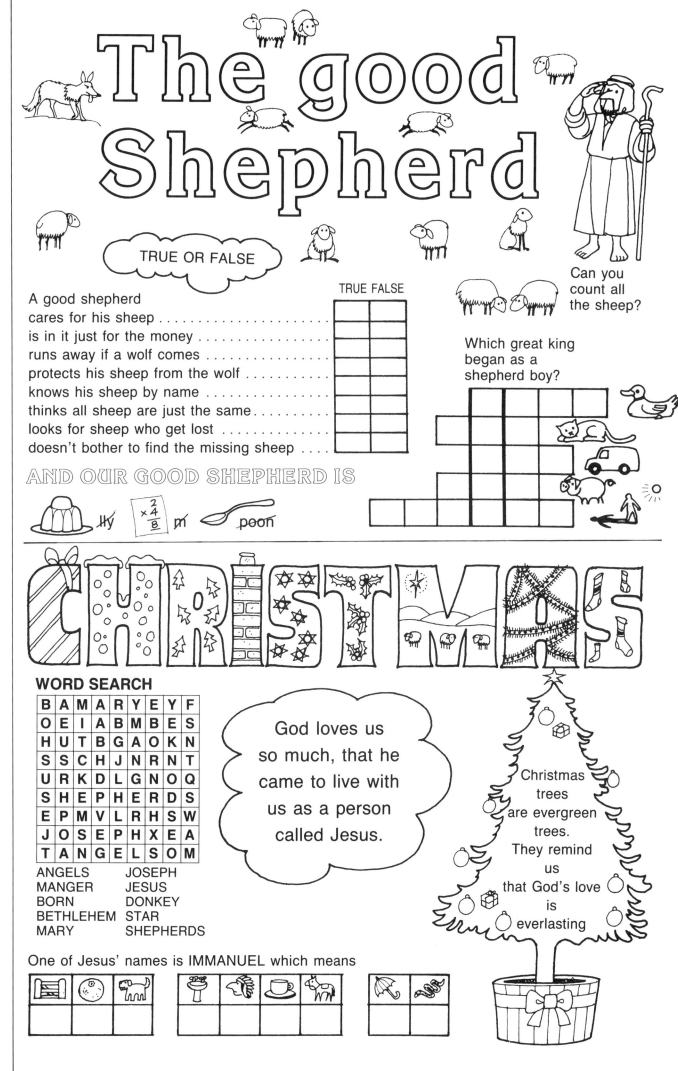

TRUE OR FALSE

	TRUE	FALSE
A good shepherd cares for his sheep		
is in it just for the money		
runs away if a wolf comes		
protects his sheep from the wolf		
knows his sheep by name		
thinks all sheep are just the same		
looks for sheep who get lost		
doesn't bother to find the missing sheep		

Can you count all the sheep?

Which great king began as a shepherd boy?

AND OUR GOOD SHEPHERD IS

CHRISTMAS

WORD SEARCH

B	A	M	A	R	Y	E	Y	F
O	E	I	A	B	M	B	E	S
H	U	T	B	G	A	O	K	N
S	S	C	H	J	N	R	N	T
U	R	K	D	L	G	N	O	Q
S	H	E	P	H	E	R	D	S
E	P	M	V	L	R	H	S	W
J	O	S	E	P	H	X	E	A
T	A	N	G	E	L	S	O	M

ANGELS   JOSEPH
MANGER   JESUS
BORN   DONKEY
BETHLEHEM   STAR
MARY   SHEPHERDS

God loves us so much, that he came to live with us as a person called Jesus.

Christmas trees are evergreen trees. They remind us that God's love is everlasting

One of Jesus' names is IMMANUEL which means